I0752418

LAVAROW / SENTENCES

To make sentences in the present tense, use something from column 1 and then from columns 2 + 3 together, and/or column 4.

1

- I am — Ydh esov vy
- You (s.) are — Ydh esta
- He is — Yma ev
- She is — Yma hi
- We are — Ydh eson ni
- You (pl.) are — Ydh esough hwi
- They are — Ydh esons i
- Jenna is — Yma Jenna
- The car is — Yma an car

2

(link word):

ow *(before consonants)*

owth *(before vowels)*

3

- tos omma coming over
- kul tesenn making a cake
- eva te drinking tea
- tybri hansel eating breakfast
- mos dhe'n davern going to the pub
- kavos kowas having a shower
- miras orth an bellwolok watching TV
- koslowes orth ilow listening to music
- kwari playing (a game)
- redya an paper reading the paper
- prena boes food shopping
- lavurya working
- skrifa lyther writing a letter
- tannvon e-bost sending an e-mail

4

- war an voes on the table
- war an fordh on the way
- y'n kyttrin on the bus
- y'n amari in the cupboard
- y'n dre in the town
- y'n lowarth in the garden
- orth an daras by the door
- ryb an chi by the house
- yn-dan an new under the sink

Cornish in your pocket

Language basics

y lolfa

(m) = masculine
(f) = feminine
(s) = singular
(pl) = plural
lit. = literally

© Y Lolfa Cyf., 2021

with special thanks to Dr Talat Chaudhri
for translation

ISBN: 978-1-78461-876-6

Printed and published in Wales by
Y Lolfa Cyf., Talybont, Ceredigion SY24 5HE
01970 832 304
ylolfa@ylolfa.com

For more Cornish learning materials, browse
https://gocornish.org/learn-cornish/

YNGANU / PRONUNCIATION

a	can be short as in "man", or long as *a* in "father"
b	*b*
c	*k* as in "kite"
ch	as in "cherry"
d	*d*
dh	as *th* in "that"
e	can be short as in "ten", or long as *ai* in "hair"
f	*f*
g	as in "got"
gh	as *ch* in "loch"
h	*h*
i	can be short as in "win", or long as *ee* in "see"
j	as in "jar"
k	as in "kite"
l	*l*
m	*m*
n	*n*
o	can be short as in "lot" or long as *ou* in "four"
p	*p*
r	as in "run"
s	as in "sun" at the start of a word; as *z* in "zoo" elsewhere
sh	as in "shine"
t	*t*
th	as in "thin"
u	like a long i, as *ee* in "see" but with rounder lips
v	*v*
w	*w*
y	as *ee* in "teen" or as *i* in "win"

GORHEMMYNNADOW / GREETINGS

Dydh da	Good day, Hello
Dewgh yn-chi	Come in
Fatla genes?	How are you?
Dynnargh	Welcome
Myttin da	Good morning
Dydh da	Good afternoon (*lit.* Good day)
Gorthugher da	Good evening
Nos da	Good night
Mar pleg	Please
Meur ras	Thanks/Thank you very much
Oll an gwella	All the best
Dew genes	Goodbye
Pub bolonjedh da	Best wishes
Gav dhymm	Excuse me
Drog yw genev	I'm sorry
(My a wra) dha weles	(I'll) see you
Keslowena	Congratulations
Penn-bloedh Lowen	Happy Birthday
Nadelek Lowen	Merry Christmas
Bledhen Nowedh Da	Happy New Year
Yeghes da!	Cheers! (*lit.* Good health!)

PUB DYDH / EVERYDAY

Ydh esof vy ow tysky Kernewek I'm learning Cornish

Pyth yw ____ yn Kernewek? What's ___ in Cornish?

Fatel leverowgh why ____ yn Kernewek? How do you say ___ in Cornish?

A rewgh why ____ dhymm? May I have ...?

...hanafas te... a cup of tea

...dew de... two teas

...hanafas koffi... a cup of coffee

...dew goffi... two coffees

...gwedrennas dowr... a glass of water

...pinta korev... a pint of beer

...gwedrennas gwin gwyn... a glass of white wine

...gwedrennas gwin rudh... a glass of red wine

...an rol-voes... the menu

...tesenn... cake

...an reken... the bill

Ple'ma an privedhyow? Where is the toilet?

AWEL / WEATHER

Note: you refer to the weather as 'she'.

Splann yw hi	It's fine
Tomm yw hi	It's hot
Yeyn yw hi	It's cold
Komolek yw hi	It's cloudy
Glyb yw hi	It's wet
Sygh yw hi	It's dry
Niwlek yw hi	It's foggy
Garow yw hi	It's stormy
Gwynsek yw hi	It's windy
Yma an howl ow splanna	It's sunny
Yma glaw ow kodha	It's raining
Yma ergh ow kodha	It's snowing

SESONYOW / SEASONS

gwenten	spring
hav	summer
kynnyav	autumn
gwav	winter

Cledh (N)

Howlsedhes (W) — **Howldrehevel** (E)

Deghow (S)

NYVEROW / NUMBERS

1 onan
2 dew (m)/diw (f)
3 tri (m)/teyr (f)
4 peswar (m) /peder (f)
5 pymp
6 hwegh
7 seyth
8 eth
9 naw
10 deg
11 unnek
12 dewdhek
13 tredhek
14 peswardhek
15 pymthek
16 hwetek
17 seytek
18 etek
19 nawnsek
20 ugens
21 onan warn ugens
30 deg warn ugens
31 unnek warn ugens
40 dew-ugens
50 hanterkans
51 onan ha hanterkans
100 kans
101 kans hag onan
110 kans ha deg
111 kans hag unnek
200 dew gans
1000 mil

ARGHANS / MONEY

Pygemmys a gost? How much does it cost?

£ **puns** pound
p **diner** penny

Tri funs three pounds
Teyr dinerenn three pence

MOS / GOING

mos dhe going to

mos dhe'n gwerthjyow going to the shops

mos y'n kyttrin going by bus

Ydh esov vy ow mos dhe'n lavur a-vorow
I'm going to work tomorrow

Ydh esons i ow mos dhe'n dre
They're going to town

NAGHA / SAYING YOU'RE NOT

Put 'Ny' before the verb (or 'Nyns' before some vowels):

Ny wonn vy I don't know

NOTE THESE:

Nyns usy hi ow tyski Kernewek
She isn't learning Cornish

Nyns esons i ow mos dhe'n dre
They're not going to town

Ny gonvedhav vy I don't understand

TABEL TRELYANSOW HA NEBES REWLYS
THE MUTATIONS TABLE AND SOME BASIC RULES

	Medhel **Soft**	Hwethys **Aspirate**	Kales **Hard**	Kemmyskys **Mixed**
P →	B	F		
T →	D	Th		
K →	G	H		
B →	V		P	F
D →	Dh		T	T
G →	–		K	H
Ch →	J			
M →	V			F
	⇩ *After* a, dre, dhe, yn-dan, dew, diw, mil, war *After* an (the) – *(f) (s) nouns only and (m) (pl) nouns when people* *Adjectives after (f) (s) nouns and (m) (pl) nouns when people* *After* dha (your), y (his)	⇩ *After* tri/teyr (3) *After* hy (her) *After* ow (my) *After* aga (their)	⇩ *After* ow (link word) *After* mar (if)	⇩ *After* p'eur (when) *After* ple (where) *After* 'th (your) *And with some conjunctions and link words before verbs*

MISYOW / MONTHS

Genver	Jan	Gortheren	Jul
Hwevrer	Feb	Est	Aug
Meurth	Mar	Gwyngala	Sep
Ebrel	Apr	Hedra	Oct
Me	May	Du	Nov
Metheven	Jun	Kevardhu	Dec

P'eur yma dha benn-bloedh jy?
When is your birthday?
Dhe'n pympes a vis Meurth
On the fifth of March

DYDHYOW AN SEYTHEN / DAYS OF THE WEEK

dy-Lun	Monday
dy-Meurth	Tuesday
dy-Mergher	Wednesday
dy-Yow	Thursday
dy-Gwener	Friday
dy-Sadorn	Saturday
dy-Sul	Sunday

AN EUR / TIME

un eur	1 o'clock
diw eur	2 o'clock
teyr eur	3 o'clock
deg eur	10 o'clock
unnek eur	11 o'clock
dewdhek eur	12 o'clock
Py eur yw?	What time is it?
Diw eur yw.	It's two o'clock.
Kwartrenn wosa deg yw.	It's quarter past ten.
Hanter wosa teyr yw.	It's half past three.
Kwartrenn dhe bymp yw.	It's quarter to five.
hanterdydh	midday
hanternos	midnight

P'EUR? / WHEN?

lemmyn	now	y'n penseythen	at the weekend
hedhyw	today	y'n seythen nessa	next week
an myttin-ma	this morning	y'n mis nessa	next month
dohajydh	this afternoon	y'n mis diwetha	last month
haneth	tonight	hevlena	this year
de	yesterday	warlena	last year
nyhewer	last night		
a-vorow	tomorrow		
kyns pell	before long		

GOVYNNOW / QUESTIONS

Put these at the beginning of the sentence:

Pandra? What?	Prag? Why?
Piw? Who?	Fatel? How?
P'eur? When?	Ple? Where?

e.g. Pandr' esta ow kul? What are you doing?
Prag esta ow kul tesenn? Why are you making a cake?
Piw usy ow kwari? Who's playing?
Fatel woer Jenna? How does Jenna know?
P'eur tons i? When are they coming?
Ple eson ni ow mos? Where are we going?

GORTHYB "YA" / ANSWERING "YES"

Answering questions in the present tense

To answer questions starting with "are you/is he/are they", etc., you say "I am/ he is/they are" etc.

Esov	Yes, I am
Usy	Yes, he/she/it is
Eson	Yes, we/they are

e.g. Usy hi ow tos? Usy. Is she coming? Yes, she is.

ATEB "NA" / ANSWERING "NO"

Na	No
Nag esov	No, I'm not
Nag usy	No, he/she/it isn't
Nag eson	No, we/they aren't
Martesen	Maybe

e.g. Esta ow tos haneth? Nag esov.
Are you coming tonight? No, I'm not.

GORHEMMYNNOW / COMMANDS

Deus	Come (s)
Dewgh	Come (pl)
Ke	Go (s)
Ewgh	Go (pl)
Pren	Buy (s)
Prenewgh	Buy (pl)
Red	Read (s)
Redyewgh	Read (pl)
Myr	Look (s)
Myrewgh	Look (pl)
Na wra	Don't (s)
Na wrewgh	Don't (pl)

hynwyn gwann /adjectives

euthek	awful
drog	bad
teg	beautiful, lovely, pretty
bras	big
skwithus	boring
bysi	busy
a bris isel	cheap
skentel	clever
kales	difficult, hard
a-brys	early
es	easy
koeth	excellent
kostek	expensive
a vri	famous
pell	far
uskis	fast
hwarthus	funny
da	good
lowen	happy
ughel	high
poesek	important
hegar	kind
diwedhes	late
hir	long, tall
isel	low
kul	narrow
ogas	near
hweg	nice
koth	old
boghosek	poor
golusek	rich
trist	sad
berr	short
lent	slow
byghan	small
medhel	soft
ewn	straight
gocky	stupid
hager	ugly
efan	wide
yowynk	young

verbow /verbs

gorthebi	answer
dos dhe	arrive
govyn	ask
gallos	be able
prena	buy
gelwel	call
yskynna	climb
degea	close
dos	come
kegina	cook
eva	drink
lewya	drive
dybri	eat
enjoya	enjoy
gorfenna	finish
neyja	fly
ankevi	forget
kavos	get
ri	give
mos	go
dismygi	guess
hwarvos	happen
kasa	hate
klewes	hear
gwitha	keep
dyski	learn
gasa	leave
kara	like, love
goslowes	listen
bewa	live
mires	look
kelli	lose
metya	meet
gwaya	move
ygeri	open
pe	pay
gwari	play (game)
seni	play (music)
ommasaya	practise
redya	read
perthi kov	remember
dasweles	revise
leverel	say
gweles	see
gwertha	sell
danvon	send
kana	sing
esedha	sit
koska	sleep
kewsel	speak
lytherenna	spell
kemeres	take
prederi	think
treylya	translate
konvedhes	understand
usya	use
difuna	wake
kerdhes	walk
mires	watch
gwiska	wear
gwaynya	win
oberi	work
skrifa	write

Cornish in your pocket

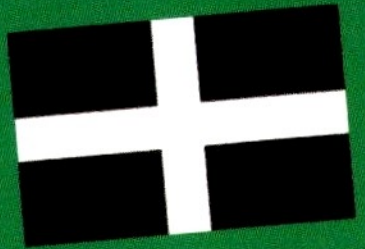

Basic words

y lolfa

teylu/family

modrep	aunt
mab/maw	boy
broder	brother
broder dre lagha	brother-in-law
keniterow	cousin (f)
kenderow	cousin (m)
myrgh	daughter/girl
gohydh	daughter-in-law
tas	father
hwegron	father-in-law
tas-gwyn	grandfather
mamm-wyn	grandmother
gour	husband
mamm	mother
hweger	mother-in-law
noy	nephew
nith	niece
kar	parent
hwoer	sister
hwoer dre lagha	sister-in-law
mab	son
deuv	son-in-law
les-vroder	stepbrother
les-vyrgh	stepdaughter
les-tas	stepfather
les-vamm	stepmother
les-hwoer	stepsister
les-vab	stepson
ewnter	uncle
gwreg	wife

an korf/the body

ufern	ankle
bregh	arm
keyn	back
tin	backside
torr	belly
bogh	cheek
brest	chest
skovarn	ear
penelin	elbow
lagas	eye
abrans	eyebrow
bys	finger
troes	foot
tal	forehead
gols	hair
leuv	hand
penn	head
penglin	knee
gar	leg
gweus	lip
ganow	mouth
konna	neck
troen	nose
skoedh	shoulder
dans	tooth
konna bregh	wrist

dillas/clothes

kota	coat
pows	dress
jerkyn	jacket
gwlanek	jumper
kota glaw	raincoat
krys	shirt
eskis/eskisyow	shoe/shoes
lavrek kott	shorts
losten	skirt
lodrik/lodrigow	sock/socks
sewt	suit
krys-T	T-shirt
lavrek	trousers

liwyow/colours

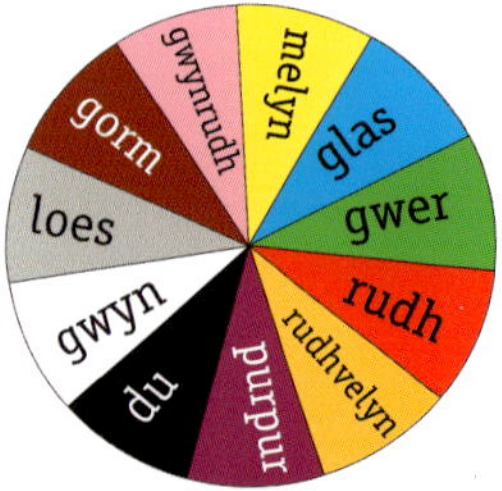

sportow / sports

athletek	athletics
pel-ganstell	basketball
boksusi	boxing
yskynna	climbing
kennerther	coach
krycket	cricket
diwrosa	cycling
pel-droes	football
gwari	game
golf	golf
hocki	hockey
pel-roes	netball
breusydh	referee
kylghyow	rounders
revya	rowing
reugbi	rugby
resek	running
skorya	score
skia	skiing
mordardha	surfing
neuvya	swimming
tennis	tennis
bagas	team

soedhow / jobs

gwarier	actor
awtour	author
gweythor chi	builder
kog	chef
dynsor	dentist
medhek	doctor
lewyer	driver
penskrifer	editor
tiek	farmer
pyskador	fisherman
lowarther	gardener
gour chi	house husband
gwreg chi	housewife
gwithyas bewnans	lifeguard
dyghtyer	manager
klavjior	nurse
gwythwas kres	police officer
lytherwas	postman
skrifennyas	secretary
gwerthjior	shopkeeper
dyskador	teacher, tutor
stenor	tinner, tin miner
diweyth	unemployed
servyas	waiter
gweythor	worker

drehevyansow / buildings

arghanti	bank
koffiji	café
kastell	castle
chapel	chapel
eglos	church
sinema	cinema
kleub	club
kolji	college
gweythva	factory
bargen tir	farm
rannji	flat
hel	hall
klavji	hospital
ostel	hotel
lyverva	library
gwithti	museum
soedhva	office
tavern	pub
boesti	restaurant
skol	school
gwerthji	shop
gorsav	station
medhegva	surgery
poll-neuvya	swimming pool
gwariva	theatre
pennskol	university

enyvales/animals

edhen	bird
tarow	bull
leugh	calf
kath	cat
bugh	cow
ki	dog
mul	donkey
hos	duck
owrbysk	goldfish
goedh	goose
hogh Gyni	guinea pig
hamster	hamster
yar	hen
margh	horse
oen	lamb
logosen	mouse
papynjay	parrot
hogh	pig
konin	rabbit
davas	sheep
sarf	snake

ynchy/home

stevel-omwolghi	bathroom
gwely	bed
chambour	bedroom
kader	chair
jynn-amonytya	computer
stevel-howl	conservatory
amari	cupboard
desk	desk
stevel-dhybri	dining room
daras	door
trog-tenna	drawer
karrji	garage
lowarth	garden
chi	house
kegin	kitchen
esedhva	lounge
mirour	mirror
pellgowser	phone
stevel	room
kowas	shower
new	sink
sofa	sofa
moes	table
pellwolok	television
seghador dillas	tumble dryer
dilasva	wardrobe
jynn-golghi	washing machine
fenester	window

y'n gegin/in the kitchen

aval	apple
bakken	bacon
kig bewin	beef
korev	beer
bara	bread
hansel	breakfast
tesen gales	biscuit
bolla	bowl
amanyn	butter
tesen	cake
karetys	carrots
keus	cheese
kig yar	chicken
asklos	chips
choklet	chocolate
koffi	coffee
hanaf	cup
keurri	curry
lestri	dishes
jynn golchi lestri	dishwasher
oy	egg
pysk	fish
bleus	flour
forgh	fork
rewer	freezer
yeynell	fridge
ffroeth	fruit
gwedren	glass
dehen rew	ice cream

dyski/learning

art	art
kuntelles	assembly
lyver	book
boesti	canteen
klass	class
Kernewek	Cornish
kors	course
Sawsnek	English
apposyans	exam
hel sport	gym
hel	hall
istori	history
ober tre	homework
dyskans	lesson
mathematek	mathematics
ilow	music
paper	paper
kwestyon	question
lavar	sentence
oberenn	task
euryador	timetable
ger	word

termyn rydh/free time

treth	beach
kampya	to camp
klappya	to chat
keskan	concert
byrla	to cuddle
hanafas	cuppa
donsya	to dance
e-bost	e-mail
fylm	film
gwari	fun
kerdhes	to go for a walk
goelyow	holiday
an gwias	the internet
hwerthin	to laugh
syger	leisure
goslowes orth ilow	to listen to music
an nowodhow	the news
payntya	to paint
kevewi	party
pinta	pint
gwari gwariow video	to play video games
diskwitha	to relax
omhowla	to sunbathe
twitya	to tweet
myras orth an bellwolok	to watch TV

sugen	juice
kalter	kettle
kollel	knife
kig oen	lamb
torth	loaf
li	lunch
kruskyn	mug
oyl	oil
owraval	orange
forn	oven
pasti	pasty
puber	pepper
plat	plate
kig mogh	pork
patatys	potatoes
podyn	pudding
salad	salad
holan	salt
baramanyn	sandwich
padell-dhorn	saucepan
kowl	soup
lo	spoon
syvi	strawberries
sugra	sugar
soper	supper
te	tea
kras	toast
boes losowek	vegetarian food
dowr	water
gwin	wine

lavurya/travel

ayren	aeroplane
diwros	bike
pons	bridge
kyttrin	bus
karr	car
sita	city
gwlas	country
ardak	delay
vyaj	journey
bownder	lane
kledh	left
kert	lorry
mildir	mile
hyns	path
deghow	right
fordh	road
arwoedh	sign
stret	street
tokyn	ticket
tre	town
tren	train
karven	van
gwig	village